Practise Punctuation
Book 1

Hilda King
Patricia Wyatt

Egon Publishers Ltd
618 Leeds Road, Outwood
Wakefield WF1 2LT
www.egon.co.uk

Practise Punctuation ~ Book 1

ISBN: 978-1873533 28 4
First published: 1995
Revised: 2001 and 2006
Egon Edition: 2015

Egon Publishers Ltd
618 Leeds Road, Outwood
Wakefield   WF1 2LT
Tel/FAX: 01924 871697
www.egon.co.uk
information@egon.co.uk

Copyright © Hilda King

All rights reserved. This book is sold subject on the condition that it shall not, by way of trade use, be copied for resale, hire, loan, or given without charge by the purchaser to a third party without prior permission of the publisher. No part of this publication may be reproduced, in part or whole, stored in a retrieval system or transmitted in any form or by any means, electronic, mechanical, recording or otherwise, without prior permission of the publisher. All pages in this book can be photocopied for educational purposes only within a school or educational establishment. No limitation is placed on the number of copies produced within the school or educational establishment.

There are 3 books in this series:

978-1873533 59 8	Practise Punctuation – Book 0
978-1873533 28 4	Practise Punctuation – Book 1
978-1873533 29 1	Practise Punctuation – Book 2

Practise Punctuation ~ Book 1

Contents

	Pages
Capital letters and full stops	5 - 18
Question mark	19 - 21
Comma	22 - 27
Exclamation mark	30 - 31
Apostrophe	
Omission apostrophe	32 - 35
Belonging apostrophe	37 - 44
Revision pages:	
Commas	28
Capital letters, question marks	29
Omission apostrophe, commas	36
Belonging apostrophe	45
Notes	47
Answers	48 - 49

Practise Punctuation ~ Book 1 ~ Key stage 2

About this book

This book, together with Book 0 and Book 2, aims to meet the requirements of the National Curriculum.

Punctuation rules are clearly defined in each section. Many diverse activities have been included to consolidate comprehension, learning and differentiation.

Pupils should be encouraged to read their work aloud. This will help them to understand the connection between the pauses, emphasis and intonation in the spoken words and the punctuation marks of the written sentences.

Punctuation marks included in Book 1 are: full stops, question marks, commas, exclamation marks and the possessive and omission apostrophes. There are also many varied exercises using capital letters in different ways. Notes for teachers are indicated by asterisks and are intended to highlight areas which may need clarification or additional guidance. These notes are on page 47.

There are no hard and fast rules for the use of full stops in abbreviations. For this reason, this topic has not been covered.

The Sassoon typeface has been used for all the worksheets. Book 1 extends and develops the activities in Book 0 and meets the requirements of Key Stages 2 and 3.

Practise Punctuation ~ Book 1 ~ Key stage 2

A Capital letters and full stops

> A sentence begins with a capital letter
> and ends with a full stop.
>
> It always has at least one verb.
>
> e.g. We like to take our dog for a walk.

**When you write your own sentences always remember these rules.
Add capital letters and full stops to each sentence below.**

1. my cat likes to drink milk

2. we often go camping in the holidays

3. there are thirty children in my class

4. it was too cold to swim in the sea

5. we saw the fox under the tree

6. one day we all went for a bicycle ride

7. sometimes it snows in winter

8. my friend cut her finger on the knife

9. we had a lovely time at the fair

10. it is dangerous to play with matches

11. we are going for a long walk today

12. my sister is very good on the computer

© (HK) HILDA KING EDUCATIONAL

A Capital letters and full stops

> **Remember:**
> a sentence begins with a capital letter
> and ends with a full stop.
>
> It always has at least one verb.

**When you write your own sentences always remember these rules.
Add capital letters and full stops to make two sentences in each line.**

1. my sister likes fish and chips my brother likes hamburgers

2. turn the music down it is too loud

3. it is cold today we will need our coats

4. the horse stepped on my foot it hurt

5. my stepbrother comes home today we are going to meet him

6. blow out the match it will burn your finger

7. we did our homework we then played football

8. put the ice cream in the fridge it will melt

9. my pen is blue his pen is black

10. our dog was ill we took him to see the vet

11. today is a holiday we hope that it will not rain

12. come quickly our cat has been found

A Capital letters and full stops

Below is a passage of text. Rewrite it as four sentences, putting in the capital letters and full stops.

elephants have trunks they do not use their trunks like straws they fill only the tip of the trunk with water they spray the water into their mouths

Below is a passage of text. Rewrite it as four sentences, putting in the capital letters and full stops.

a whale is a mammal there are eighty kinds of whale an adult sperm whale may have a brain which weighs nine kilograms we do not know if this means that the whale is very clever

Below is a passage of text. Rewrite it as seven sentences, putting in the capital letters and full stops.

a snake has two skins the outside skin is hard and scaly and does not grow the inside skin is soft and does grow the snake, as it grows bigger, sheds its outer skin the inside skin is then outside this skin dries and becomes hard a new inner skin grows

Practise Punctuation ~ Book 1 ~ Key stage 2

A Capital letters and full stops

Remember:
the word 'I' is always a capital letter

e.g. "I want to go swimming."

Rewrite the following sentences with 'I' instead of 'i' and put in the capital letters and full stops.

1. that is not where i want to go

2. he told me that i was good at football

3. that is the game i would like for my computer

4. i ran very fast in the race

5. i told my friend that i could go to her house for tea

Change the 'you' to 'I' and add the capital letters and full stops. There are two sentences in some of the examples.

1. you will see john at sarah's house

2. you always wear blue shoes

3. you can go to her party

4. he read that book you read it first

5. you love cakes she likes cheese

6. you do not turn left you turn right

Practise Punctuation ~ Book 1 ~ Key stage 2

A   *Capital letters and full stops*

> **Remember:**
> always use a capital letter for a name.
>
> e.g. Joshua, Aisha.

Add capital letters and full stops to make two sentences in each line.

1. i put on my music john did not like it

2. we went to the fair I had a ride on the dodgems

3. i go to school on the bus ann walks to school

4. please come to my house it is harry's birthday

5. i had lunch with gill david did not

6. the bell rang susan ran to open the door

7. linda began to play the trumpet peter left the room

8. goldfish do not bite hamsters do

9. i am going skating janet said that she would come, too

10. that house is said to have a ghost i do not believe in ghosts

11. i love fish chips give me tummy ache

12. i am going to see my uncle tom will come with me

A Capital letters and full stops

> **Remember:**
> always use a capital letter for a place name.
>
> e.g. England, India, Manchester, Brisbane.

Below is a passage of text. Rewrite it as five sentences, putting in the capital letters and full stops.

james was a king twice he was james VI of scotland he later became james I of england he was clever and witty and good with money he was also short and fat

Below is a passage of text. Rewrite it as eight sentences, putting in the capital letters and full stops.

sharks live in the sea there are many stories about sharks people in australia have to be careful when they swim some beaches have shark nets to protect swimmers from attack the great white shark is one of the most dangerous it has been known to bite off arms and legs it has even killed people i have never seen a great white shark

Practise Punctuation ~ Book 1 ~ Key stage 2

A Capital letters and full stops

> **Remember:**
> **always use a capital letter for the name of:**
> **a street or a road**   e.g. Church Lane
> **a building**   e.g. Westminster Abbey
> **a train or bus station**   e.g. King's Cross
> **an airport**   e.g. Stansted Airport

Add the capital letters and full stops.

1. peter lives in bridge street

2. i went to church road to visit auntie jess

3. there are soldiers in front of buckingham palace

4. he drove to gatwick airport to see his uncle bill

5. catch the bus at victoria station

6. the statue of nelson is in trafalgar square

Add the capital letters and arrange the sentences in the right order.

i went on a plane to france

i went to milton bus station

i left my house in mill street

i went by bus to birmingham airport

A Capital letters and full stops

Rewrite the passage below in five sentences, using upper and lower case letters. Begin each sentence with a capital letter and end each with a full stop. You will also need to keep some capital letters in other places.

MY SISTER ALICE IS TWO SHE WENT SHOPPING WITH MY MUM MY MUM IS CALLED PAT WHILE THEY WERE SHOPPING ALICE ATE A WHOLE BAG OF RAISINS MY MUM SAID THIS HAD KEPT HER QUIET

Do the same with this passage. There are four sentences this time.

MY NAME IS SAM I LIVE IN GREEN STREET, OLDHAM I HAVE A BROTHER CALLED JAMES AND A SISTER CALLED ANNE MY DAD WORKS IN MANCHESTER

Do the same with this passage. There are four sentences this time.

I WENT TO PARIS I MET MY COUSIN PHILIPPE HE TOOK ME TO SEE THE EIFFEL TOWER FROM THE TOP OF THE EIFFEL TOWER I SAW PARIS

A Capital letters and full stops

Rewrite the passage below in seven sentences. Remember to put in all the full stops and capital letters.

KOALAS COME FROM AUSTRALIA THEY FEED ON GUM LEAVES THEY NEVER DRINK WATER THEY GET THE JUICE FROM THE GUM LEAVES THEY LOOK VERY SWEET BUT THEY HAVE LONG SHARP CLAWS KOALAS USED TO BE HUNTED FOR THEIR FUR THEY ARE NOW PROTECTED ANIMALS

Do the same with this passage. There are ten sentences this time.

I LIVE IN ASH DRIVE, OXFORD THE JOHN RADCLIFFE HOSPITAL IS NEAR OUR HOUSE I WENT ON A SCHOOL TRIP TO HOLLAND I WENT WITH MRS JONES AND MY CLASS WE WENT BY COACH AND BOAT MRS JONES TOOK A BUCKET THIS WAS A GOOD IDEA BECAUSE WAYNE WAS SICK WE SAW LOTS OF FLOWERS AND WINDMILLS IN HOLLAND IT WAS VERY LATE WHEN WE GOT BACK TO OXFORD WE WERE ALL VERY TIRED

Practise Punctuation ~ Book 1 ~ Key stage 2

A Capital letters and full stops

> Remember:
> always use a capital letter for:
> days of the week   e.g. Monday
> months of the year   e.g. December

Days of the week
Add the capital letters.

_ onday,   _uesday,   _ednesday,   _hursday,   _riday
_aturday,   _unday

Months of the year, add the capital letters.

_anuary,   _ebruary,   _arch,   _pril,   _ay,   _une,   _uly,
_ ugust,   _eptember, _ctober, _ovember,   _ecember

Quiz
Find the five months from the clues. Then find the day of the week.

1. The month with two Bank holidays _____

2. The tenth month _____

3. Leaves fall and fireworks explode in _____

4. Christmas comes in this month _____

5. Before September, but after July _____

6. Use the first letter of each answer, add a sixth letter and you will have a day of the week. _____

© HK HILDA KING EDUCATIONAL

Practise Punctuation ~ Book 1 ~ Key stage 2

A Capital letters and full stops

> **Remember:**
> always use a capital letter for special days:
> e.g. Christmas Day, Easter Day, Good Friday,
> Ramadan, Mother's Day, Hanukkah,
> Chinese New Year, Diwali.

Add capital letters and full stops to make two sentences from each line.

1. i am going to the match on saturday

2. next week we celebrate hanukkah

3. i am going to venice in july

4. i think that easter is in march this year

5. gita told me that ramadan is in october

6. in australia christmas is in the summer

7. i have bought my mother a rose for mother's day

8. people put on lights in their homes to celebrate diwali

9. we have chocolate eggs on easter sunday

10. my birthday is on thursday

11. thanksgiving day is in november

12. we are going away on august bank holiday monday

© HK HILDA KING EDUCATIONAL

A Capital letters and full stops

Remember:
*always use a capital letter for:
- **titles of books** — e.g. Black Beauty
- **titles of poems** — e.g. The Jabberwocky
- **names of newspapers** — e.g. The Times
- **titles of plays, films** — e.g. The Lion King

Add capital letters and full stops to each sentence below.

1. my mum reads the bible every day

2. we had to learn a passage from macbeth

3. my favourite film is casablanca

4. the poem the rime of the ancient mariner tells an exciting story

5. my dad always reads the daily telegraph

6. the beatles sang please, please me

7. at christmas we sang silent night

8. i have the video of aladdin

9. we read about swan lake in the observer

10. i went to see starlight express by andrew lloyd webber

* See page 47, note (i)

A Capital letters and full stops

> **Remember:**
> **always use a capital letter for deities:**
> e.g. God, Jesus, Christ, Allah;
> **and for titles:** e.g. Princess Margaret
> Sir Winston Churchill
> President Mandela
> Doctor Jones

Add the capital letters and full stops.

1. the queen is married to prince philip

2. peter was one of the disciples of jesus

3. his royal highness prince charles will go to the wedding

4. i saw the president of the united states

> **Remember:**
> *if a title is <u>not</u> followed by a name, do <u>not</u> use a capital letter.
> e.g. <u>D</u>octor <u>S</u>mith lives next door,
> but I go to see another <u>d</u>octor if I am ill.

Add the capital letters and full stops.

1. all the generals had dinner at general patton's house

2. mr king played golf with major thomas

3. sir edmund hillary climbed mount everest

4. the duke and duchess of windsor lived in paris

* See page 47, note (ii)

A Capital letters and full stops

*Rewrite this poem, putting in the capital letters.

the vulture
the vulture eats between his meals;
he very, very rarely feels
as well as you and i.

his eye is dull, his head is bald,
his neck is growing thinner,
oh! what a lesson for us all
to only eat at dinner!

by Hilaire Belloc

Rewrite the story on another sheet, putting in all the capital letters and full stops.

mrs jones is very forgetful she was coming to see me on monday it was cold because it was december before she left the house she put her purse in the fridge and the butter in her pocket she marched down the road in her slippers and came to church street she spoke to the statue of prince william and passed the new marks and spicer shop i was very worried because she was late i took my dog bonzo and went with my friend doris to find her we saw her in the cinema queue waiting to see the film lost in hyde park

*See page 47, note (iii).

The question mark

> **Remember:**
> every question must end with a question mark.
>
> e.g. What is the time?

Rewrite the questions and add the question marks.

1. How are you

2. Where is he

3. Have you done your homework

4. How much is that, please

> **Remember:**
> the question mark finishes a question.
> So the next word must begin with a capital letter.
>
> e.g. What is the time? It is ten o'clock.

Rewrite the following sentences, adding capital letters, question marks and full stops.

1. how are you i'm very well, thank you

2. can you swim i am learning and can almost swim

3. do you like cheese yes, we love it

4. where are you going on holiday we are going to ireland

The question mark ?

Remember:
special words can be used to start a question.
e.g. Where?   Where are you going?

Join the question word to the correct words to make a question.
The first question is done for you.

Question words	Matching words.
how	is your favourite lesson?
where	would you like to do on your birthday?
which	are you laughing?
whose	can I find your house?
what	is the spare bulb?
who	is it time for us to leave?
when	turn is it?
why	won the race?

(how → can I find your house?)

Write a question word at the start of each of these sentences to make a question.

1. _____ is your name?
2. _____ are you feeling?
3. _____ team will win the match?
4. _____ did you stamp on his foot?

You can turn a sentence into a question by changing the placing of the verb.   e.g. He is feeling better.   Is he feeling better?
Rewrite the sentences below as questions.

1. She has finished her homework.

2. They are going to the club tonight.

3. The teacher will give her the spelling book.

4. The boy has put stamps on the parcel.

Practise Punctuation ~ Book 1 ~ Key stage 2

The question mark ?

Write the question before each of these answers, putting in the question mark.

1. _____   It's half past two.
2. _____   I am very well.
3. _____   Turn right at the church.
4. _____   We put them in the loft.
5. _____   Yes, I shall need my umbrella.
6. _____   I took him for a long walk.
7. _____   No she has stopped crying.
8. _____   They are in the shed.

Space out these lines of letters into words and put in the capital letters, full stops and question marks. The first one is done for you.

1. canyoucomefortea   Can you come for tea?

2. whattimedoesthetrainleaveoxford

3. didyouknowthatdrcarsonwenttobuckinghampalace

4. iaskedjoantomypartyinglasgow

5. canyoushowmethestatueofwilllamblakeinbridgwater

6. whereisyourothershoe   ileftitindiana'sbag

7. thatisoneofthewaystodover   doyouknowanotherway

HILDA KING EDUCATIONAL

The comma

> **Remember:**
> the most common use of the comma is to separate different parts of a sentence. A comma makes the meaning of a sentence clearer.
>
> e.g. I can dive, swim two lengths and float.
>
> **N.B. You do not usually need a comma before or after the word 'and'.**

Rewrite the sentences adding commas to make the sense clearer.

1. When I try to sharpen a pencil the lead always breaks.

2. He jumped over the box climbed the wall bars and fell off the top.

3. We went to the flat saw Mr Blake but decided not to have it.

4. I like to go to work come home and have a bath.

5. When I went to America I saw the Grand Canyon.

6. If you go to the sales early you might find some bargains.

7. Tomorrow instead of having lessons we are going on a school trip.

8. Whenever it rains I forget my umbrella.

9. My sister will run in a marathon race next week if her cold is better.

10. As it was one hundred years since the end of the First World War there were many celebrations.

Practise Punctuation ~ Book 1 ~ Key stage 2

The comma

> **Remember:**
> **commas are used to seperate items in a list.**
> e.g. I ate cakes, jelly, sandwiches and sausages.

Rewrite the sentences below and add the commas.

1. I went to the shops and bought apples oranges and grapes.

2. We took the car to have the tyres the water and the oil checked.

3. My house has a lounge kitchen bathroom and two bedrooms.

4. You can run skip hop or jump.

5. Do not forget your ruler pencil rubber or pen.

6. I can run quickly slowly sideways or backwards.

> **Remember:**
> **a comma can change the meaning of a sentence.**
> e.g. I met Peter, Spencer and John.
> I met Peter Spencer and John.

Rewrite the sentences below and add commas where needed.

1. I met George Michael and his group.

2. I met George Michael Ben and Paul.

3. I went on the swings the roundabout and the slide with two friends called April May and June.

HILDA KING EDUCATIONAL

The comma

> **Remember:**
> **a comma is used when adding a name.**
> e.g. The driver, Mr Rashid, is tall.

Rewrite the sentences below and add the commas.

1. I saw the two largest dogs Rocco and Samson chasing the cat.

2. One of my teachers Miss Jones has a loud voice.

3. The well-known children's book Heidi is set in Switzerland.

4. Our next-door neighbour Mr. Edwards has ten pet rats.

5. One of the most famous paintings in the world the Mona Lisa is in Paris.

6. The film about a pet otter Ring of Bright Water is very sad.

> **Remember:**
> **a comma helps to make a meaning clearer.**
> e.g. It's time to eat, Mary.

Rewrite the sentences below and add commas where needed.

1. I went to hear a group play Susan.

2. Did you know Patrick Jean?

3. I went to feed Bilbo the sea lion John.

The comma

> **Remember:**
> **the comma is used when adding a description.**
>
> e.g. Lucy, a fluffy, gentle cat, likes crisps.

Rewrite these sentences and add capital letters, commas, and full stops.

1. janice a tall pretty girl won the race

2. the river trent a large river in england is very wide in parts

3. the clown a funny fat man had a white face and a red nose

4. the match watched by twenty thousand people took place at wembley

5. julius caesar a powerful roman soldier invaded england

6. the prince a young and handsome man married a duchess

7. the lion a bold and proud animal is known as the king of the beasts

8. the cave so deep and narrow was dangerous for potholers

9. the bride's dress being made of pure silk showed all the creases

10. The apple tree although old and gnarled always produces lovely apples

11. a christmas carol a famous book by charles dickens has been made into a film

Practise Punctuation ~ Book 1 ~ Key stage 2

The comma

> **Remember:**
> **the comma is used to include an added thought.**
>
> e.g. He will go, too, of course.

Rewrite these sentences and add capital letters, commas, and full stops.

1. the walk so I am told takes two hours

2. the bus by the way is always late

3. australia it is said was discovered by captain cook

4. the lions in the park I believe can be dangerous

5. you will of course win a prize

6. saturday i feel is a good day for shopping

7. whatever happens do not cross the road until it is safe

8. he parked by accident at a bus stop so he said

9. she is a good cook I think but she uses too much salt

10. the hobbit although long is an exciting book

11. peter in spite of my warning jumped into the pool

© HK HILDA KING EDUCATIONAL

Practise Punctuation ~ Book 1 ~ Key stage 2

The comma

> **Remember:**
> commas are at the end of each line of an address.
> *e.g.
>
> Miss Tracy Brown,
> 33 Hawthorn Avenue,
> Northside,
> Midcity,   MX9 5PC

Rewrite the address below, adding commas and capital letters.

miss cod   95 haddock street   fishguard   dyfed   sa26 9ny

Rewrite the address below, adding commas and capital letters.

dr pickle   the penfield surgery   hope street   stubshaw   wigan   wn3 8oj

Now write your own address below.

*See page 47, note (iv).

© HILDA KING EDUCATIONAL

The comma

Revision page

Rewrite the sentences below and add the commas.

1. The mountain bicycle although old works very well.

2. I took my trainers racquet track suit and towel with me.

3. Her hat covered in feathers stopped me from seeing the screen.

4. Ann Susan Catherine and Jane are in our group.

5. The maple tree with the sun shining on its red leaves is very pretty.

6. If you go the wrong way you will end up in a field.

7. Mr Benson the caretaker works very hard.

8. SEN Books   Home Garth   618 Leeds Road   Outwood   Wakefield   WF1 2LT

Complete the following sentences, adding commas where needed.

1. Mrs lock _____ is very strict.
2. I went to the supermarket and bought nine _____ five _____ one kilo of _____ one packet of jelly and some lemonade.
3. I was allowed to go skating even though _____ and I had not finished my essay.
4. The Empire State Building _____ is in New York.

Capital letters, commas, question marks and full stops

Revision page

Add capital letters, commas, question marks and full stops.

1. kevin keegan the well-known footballer became a manager

2. my favourite fruits are bananas apples and pears

3. the coach driver mrs. smith is a good and careful driver

4. did you know that the fat bear winnie the pooh likes honey

5. the old church saint mary's is on the corner

6. shall i buy red or white large or small potatoes from the market

7. by the way i am going to cornwall next week

8. my favourite aunt mrs spencer has a shop

9. the duke of westminster a very rich man has three children

10. did i tell you that i went to hear eric clapton sing jane

11. eros a famous statue stands in piccadilly circus

12. i saw the large tigers fred and sam at the zoo

13. the gospel of saint matthew the first book in the new testament tells of the life of jesus

*See page 47, note (v).

The exclamation mark

> **Remember:**
> an exclamation mark is used
> to express shock, surprise, delight or anger.
>
> e.g. Help!

Add exclamation marks and/or full stops.

1. Beware   Help
2. I've won first prize
3. I'm drowning   Help
4. Come quickly   The house is on fire
5. Be quiet   Dad is listening to the football results
6. Goodness   He's coming back in five minutes
7. What a dreadful film   Shall we go home and watch a video?
8. Don't panic   They've put out the fire

Make up sentences which need exclamation marks.

_____

_____

_____

Add the question marks, exclamation marks and/or full stops.

1. Sit still   I am trying to cut your toenails
2. Listen   Can you hear the thunder
3. Have you seen the Loch Ness Monster   Of course not
4. Quick   The bus is leaving
5. Can you go to camp   Gosh   No
6. It is very late   Why are you still awake
7. Goodness   Have you seen the state of the carpet
8. Quick   The cat's been sick

Practise Punctuation ~ Book 1 ~ Key stage 2

The exclamation mark

!

> **Remember:**
> an exclamation mark can also be used
> for special effect or emphasis.
>
> e.g. Come here! Your homework is a mess!
> Come here. I have a cake for you.

In each set of examples, one line needs exclamation marks and the other needs full stops. Add the correct punctuation.

1. My watch is wrong   I must get it mended
   My watch is wrong   I'm late

2. The Queen has arrived   Stand up
   The Queen has arrived   She looks very well

3. Please help me   I am looking for my hamster
   Please help   My hamster has escaped

4. Stop   The traffic light is red
   Please stop here I want to go to the bank

5. Take this tray quickly   It's too heavy
   Take this tray   There are some sandwiches on it for you

6. You can move the ladder now   The paint is dry
   Move   The ladder is falling

7. Watch out   The boat is sinking
   Watch out for the boat   It is coming into harbour

8. Wait for me please   My sandal is undone
   Wait   My foot is bleeding

9. My goodness   That was a narrow escape
   We were lucky to get tickets   The queue was very long

The apostrophe

> **Remember:**
> the omission apostrophe is used to show
> that a letter or letters are missed out.
>
> e.g. I am hot. I'm hot.
> **The apostrophe takes the place of the 'a'.**

Write the examples below in full without the apostrophes
Note: only <u>one</u> letter has been left out.

I'm _____	wasn't _____	
you're _____	didn't _____	
he's _____	couldn't _____	
she's _____	wouldn't _____	
it's _____	shouldn't _____	
we're _____	haven't _____	
they're _____	doesn't _____	
isn't _____	hasn't _____	
aren't _____	that's _____	
weren't _____	what's _____	

Make the examples below into one word by using an apostrophe.

did not _____	how is _____
here is _____	were not _____
there is _____	you are _____
where is _____	who is _____
have not _____	are not _____

Write some sentences of your own using the apostrophe.

_____
_____
_____
_____
_____

The apostrophe

> **Remember:**
> *sometimes an apostrophe can take
> the place of two or three letters.
>
> e.g. I cannot see him.   I can't see him.
> **The apostrophe takes the place of the 'n' and the 'o'.**
> e.g. I shall go.   I'll go.
> **The apostrophe takes the place of the 's' the 'h' and the 'a'.**

In the examples below change one word into two by writing out the shortened words in full. Then list the missing letters.

I'll	....I.......	..shall....	s h a	I've	_____	_____ _ _
you'll	_____	_____	_ _	you've	_____	_____ _ _
he'll	_____	_____	_ _	he's	_____	_____ _ _
she'll	_____	_____	_ _	she's	_____	_____ _ _
it'll	_____	_____	_ _	it's been	_____	_____ _ _
we'll	_____	_____	_ _ _	we've	_____	_____ _ _
they'll	_____	_____	_ _	they've	_____	_____ _ _
can't	_____	_____	_ _	who've	_____	_____ _ _

In the examples below change two words into one by adding an apostrophe. Write the word at the side.

1. I know that he will like his present.
2. I shall see you next week.
3. They cannot come with us.
4. I think that he has already left.
5. Can you tell me if they have had tea?
6. Are you sure you have had enough to eat?
7. See if it has arrived.
8. They are very good value for money.
9. He has not practised his spelling today.
10. I do not like to wear thick shirts.

*See page 47, note (vi).

The apostrophe

> **Remember:**
> sometimes an apostrophe takes
> the place of four or five letters.
>
> e.g. He would rather go now.   He'd rather go now.
> **The apostrophe takes the place of 'woul'.**

Make these examples into one word by using an apostrophe.

I should	_____	he would	_____
you would	_____	we should	_____
she would	_____	they would	_____

> **N.B.** 'o'clock' is always used for **'of the clock'**.

Rewrite the sentences below using apostrophes where possible.

1. He said that they would never agree.

2. We are wrong if that is the right answer.

3. I have never seen him look so cross.

4. We shall visit them if they have arrived.

5. I shall go if you will go, too.

6. Captain Hook said that he would meet Peter Pan at ten o'clock.

7. After breakfast we are going to see what they have made.

8. She says that they are not sure if they have seen the film.

Practise Punctuation ~ Book 1 ~ Key stage 2

The apostrophe

Look carefully at these examples with apostrophes.

a) **They're looking at the car.**
   They're is short for **they are.** It is never short for **they were.**
   Always write **they were** in full. e.g. They were looking at the car.

b) **We're happy.**
   We're is short for **we are.** It is never short for **we were.**
   Always write **we were** in full. e.g. We were happy.

c) **You're first.**
   You're is short for **you are.** It is never short for **you were.**
   Always write **you were** in full. e.g. You were first.

d) **He's last.**
   He's is short for **he is.** It is never short for **he was.**
   Always write **he was** in full. e.g. He was last.

e) **He's gone.**
   He's is also short for **he has.** It is never short for **he was.**
   Always write **he was** in full. e.g. He was gone.

Rewrite the sentences below using apostrophes where possible.

1. Hurry up! They are coming soon.

2. We knew that we were right.

3. He says we are early.

4. I think you are good at sport.

5. She was late for her piano lesson.

6. He is looking forward to the end of term.

7. She was saying that he was always on time.

The apostrophe

Revision page

Space out the words and put in the apostrophes.

1. Ithinkitsfun.   I think it's fun.
2. HesgoingtoAfrica.
3. Shehasnthadherhaircut.
4. Whatsonthetelevision?
5. Itsagoodbook.
6. Hedoesntmind.
7. Wheresmybag?
8. Werenotgoingtothefair.
9. Shesateacher.
10. Thatsagoodidea.

Letters are sometimes missed out between a noun and a verb.

e.g. The computer's broken   The computer is broken.
e.g. The computer's broken down   The computer has broken down.

Rewrite these sentences replacing the apostrophes with the missing letters.

1. My friend's sad. He's lost his pen.

2. He hasn't chosen me to play in the team.

3. They aren't willing to see if it's the right colour.

4. Who's going to see if the little boy's all right?

5. We're not sure if he's won the cup.

6. The hat's too big for him.

7. Where's the mouse? The cage's empty.

Practise Punctuation ~ Book 1 ~ Key stage 2

The belonging apostrophe

> The apostrophe has another use.
> 's is added to a noun.
> It shows that something
> or someone belongs to that noun.
> e.g. the dog's tail   the tail of the dog
> e.g. my friend's sister   the sister of my friend
> e.g. the car's driver   the driver of the car

Put the apostrophes into the examples below.

1. the horses head
2. the fishs fin
3. the cats owner
4. the lorrys tyres
5. the babys rattle
6. Williams uncle
7. my dads job
8. the teams mascot
9. Jennys bag
10. the swimming pools edge
11. the Queens head
12. the rats tail
13. the dogs dinner
14. the boys cricket bat

Make up four examples of your own

_____   _____

_____   _____

Put in the apostrophes in these sentences.

1. The wasps sting hurt the child.

2. I hope the dogs bark will not wake the neighbours.

3. It is Janes birthday next week.

4. Do you know if that is Stephens photograph?

5. Can you find your mothers purse?

© HILDA KING EDUCATIONAL

The belonging apostrophe

Rewrite these sentences using the belonging apostrophe.

1. the lid of the jar — the jar's lid.
2. the key of the shed
3. the pen of my teacher
4. the hands of my clock
5. the cover of the book
6. the legs of the chair
7. the neck of the giraffe
8. the roots of the tree
9. the brother of my uncle
10. the van of the milkman
11. the sword of the knight
12. the antlers of the deer
13. the lead of the pencil
14. the hem of the skirt
15. the throne of Queen Mary
16. the main exit of the school
17. the tail of the crow
18. the ruler of the boy
19. the friend of Paul
20. the depth of the lake

The belonging apostrophe

If a singular word already ends in s add 's.
e.g. the boss's car   Ross's house.

A Family Tree

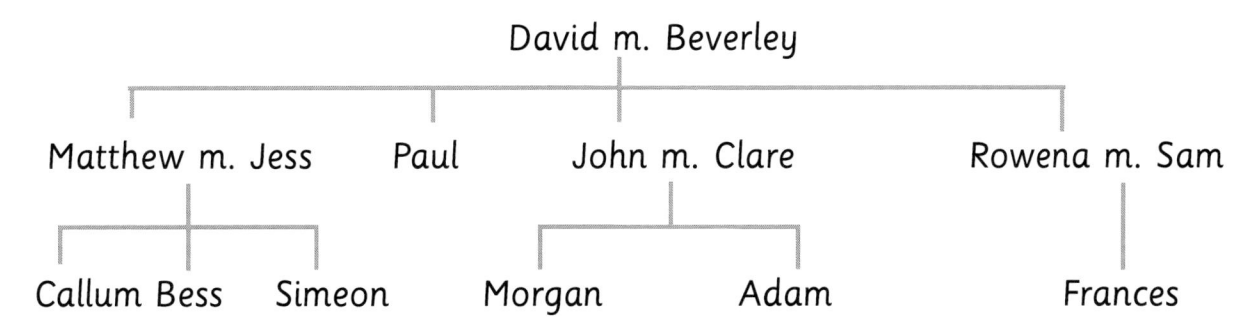

```
                    David m. Beverley
        ┌──────────────┬──────┴──────┬──────────────┐
   Matthew m. Jess    Paul      John m. Clare    Rowena m. Sam
        │                            │                  │
   ┌────┼────┐                  ┌────┴────┐             │
 Callum Bess Simeon           Morgan    Adam         Frances
```

Look at the family tree above.
Answer the questions below, adding apostrophes where needed.

1. Who is the wife of David?   David's wife is Beverley

2. Who is the husband of Beverley?   _____

3. Who is the sister of Matthew?   _____

4. Who is the daughter of Sam?   _____

5. Who is the Grandmother of Adam?   _____

6. Who is the father of Morgan?   _____

7. Who is the daughter of Jess?   _____

8. Who is the mother of Simeon?   _____

9. Who are the granddaughters of David? _____

Practise Punctuation ~ Book 1 ~ Key stage 2

The belonging apostrophe

Underline the correct examples below.

1. That chair's leg is broken
2. This is Peter's scarf
3. Where is the dogs' lead?
4. That is Joans' favourite song
5. Clare is John's sister

That chairs' leg is broken
This is Peters' scarf
Where is the dog's lead?
That is Joan's favourite song
Clare is Johns' sister

Add the apostrophe ONLY where needed in these examples.

1. That is Jeans bicycle.

2. Oxfam needs lots of blankets, warm clothes and jumpers.

3. The postmans bag was full of letters.

4. There were books and toys for sale at the bazaar.

5. James video tape was broken.

6. Peters watch was being mended, so he used Rosss.

7. The plays ending was very good.

8. Mums scales were broken so she used my sisters scales.

9. We used sticky tape to hold the pages together.

10. The chains links were very strong and held the ships anchor firmly.

Write some sentences of your own using the <u>belonging</u> apostrophe.

The belonging apostrophe

> **When a noun is plural and ends in s, es or ies add an apostrophe after the s, but do not add another s.**
>
> <u>Singular</u>   <u>Plural</u>
> e.g. a girl's shoe   girls' shoes.
> e.g. a doctor's meeting   doctors' meeting.

Write 'sing' for singular, or 'pl' for plural at the side of each example below.

1. The boys' changing rooms
2. A snake's skin
3. Ladies' handbags
4. Butterflies' wings
5. The car's engine

Make up two singular and two plural examples of your own

Add the apostrophes needed in these sentences.

1. The butchers shop is closed.
2. That is next years calendar.
3. There are birds nests in the beech trees.
4. Sandra dropped the speckled hens eggs.
5. The ships sails are red.
6. My skis clip is broken.
7. Some books covers are torn
8. The cricket teams score was high.

The belonging apostrophe

> **Some plural nouns do not end in s.**
> e.g. men, women, children
> **If a plural noun does not end in s,
> then add 's to show belonging.**
> e.g. the men's shoes;   the women's skirts.
> e.g. the children's toys.

Add the apostrophes needed in these sentences.

1. Are policemens heads the same shape as policemens helmets?
2. The peoples wishes must be carried out.
3. The womens changing rooms are cold.
4. He was a wolf in sheeps clothing.
5. Postmens bags are often heavy.
6. It is difficult to see trouts eyes.
7. The cattles lowing woke baby Jesus.

Two words, the apostrophe word followed by a noun have been put in the wrong sentences. Rewrite these sentences to make sense.

1. Women's shoes often clings to fences.

2. The style of sheep's wool is always changing.

3. The children's teacher are often red.

4. The postmen's bicycles always has an apple for lunch.

Practise Punctuation ~ Book 1 ~ Key stage 2

The belonging apostrophe

Revision page

Add the apostrophes to these sentences.

1. Williams coat is too big.
2. The boys football team did well.
3. The firemens hoses were tangled.
4. Somebodys watch has a loud alarm.
5. It was Nigels fault.
*6. Abrahams son was called Issac.
7. It is hard to find bears dens.
8. I cling to the horses mane.
9. I can remember the songs name.
10. She met me at my uncles house.

Space out the words and put in the apostrophes.

1. Harrysparrotisveryclever.

2. Isawlukesteamwin.

3. Inearlyfellsovertheccliffsedge.

4. Jacksbrotherisgoodatmaths.

5. Thethievescarbrokedown.

6. Iwenttotheladieshairdresser.

7. Thatrulersnumbersareveryfaint.

8. Aeroplanescargoesarekeptinthehold.

*See Page 47, (vii).

The apostrophe

Look carefully at the following examples.

a) **It's** my turn. **It's** means **It is**. It is my turn.

b) The pushchair has lost one of **its** wheels. **Its** means **belonging to it**.

> There is <u>no</u> apostrophe before the s.
> It is very important to remember this rule.

c) **Hers** means **belonging to her**.   **Ours** means **belonging to us**.
   Yours means **belonging to you**.   **Theirs** means **belonging to them**.

> There is <u>no</u> apostrophe before the s.

e.g. The green pencil is **hers**, the red one is **ours**,
the blue pencil is **yours** and the black one is **theirs**.

It's or its?

1. _____ time to go home now, children.
2. Have you seen the castle with _____ tall towers?
3. The school had _____ Christmas party yesterday.
4. I hope _____ not too busy.
5. Judith says that _____ always hot in India.
6. The monkey sat in _____ own dinner.

> *<u>Never</u> use an apostrophe to make words plural.

| BOOKS FOR SALE | ✓ | APPLES FOR SALE | ✓ |
| BOOK'S FOR SALE | ✗ | APPLE'S FOR SALE | ✗ |

*See Page 47, (viii).

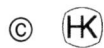

Practise Punctuation ~ Book 1 ~ Key stage 2

The apostrophes

Revision page

The apostrophe which shows letters missed out.

Add the apostrophes to these sentences.

1. Wheres my drink?
2. Its hard to understand.
3. I cant think straight.
4. I havent cleaned my teeth today.
5. We arent lucky.
6. Davids gone home.

The belonging apostrophe.

Add the apostrophes to these sentences.

1. The nurses uniform was white.
2. Flamingoes legs are very thin.
3. The conjourors trick was very clever.
4. The attics window is very small.
5. The two boys diving belts were very heavy.

Look at the sentences below.
Highlight the apostrophes in *blue* if they show letters missed out.
Highlight the apostrophes in *red* if they show belonging.

1. He isn't here.
2. Simon's shorts are very muddy.
3. Where's the picture? It's on the wall.
4. The trees' leaves are beginning to fall.
5. He wouldn't go on the Space Mountain ride.
6. The Great Wall of China's very steep.
7. Where's the rabbit's cage?
8. The photocopier won't work.
9. The yacht's cabin was quite small.
10. Is that Chris's bicycle? No. It's not.

Practise Punctuation ~ Book 1

Notes

Note (i) Page 16.
More information and explanation will be required on the use of capital letters in titles. e.g. The Wind in the Willows

Note (ii) Page 17.
More examples of this may be needed.

Note (iii) Page 18.
Poems: the use of capitals for the first letter of each line will need to be explained.

Note (iv) Page 27.
Although the address is indented this method of addressing is now less common.

Note (v) Page 29.
The use of capital letters to introduce quotations has not been included. This will be covered in Book 2.

Note (vi) Page 33
In some abbreviations an actual letter may be changed. e.g. **will not** becomes **won't**.

Note (vii) Page 43
Some names ending in s, mostly biblical or classical, sound better without an added s to show possession. e.g. Moses' basket

Note (viii) Page 44
It is very important to point out this common misuse of the apostrophe.

Practise Punctuation ~ Book 1
Answer pages

Only the answers to examples which require considerable thought have been given.

Page 38

1. That chair's leg is broken.
2. This is Peter's scarf
3. Where is the dog's lead?
4. That is Joan's favourite song.
5. Clare is John's sister.

1. That is Jean's bicycle.
2. Oxfam needs lots of blankets, warm clothes and jumpers.
3. The postman's bag was full of letters.
4. There were books and toys for sale at the bazaar.
5. James's video tape was broken.
6. Peter's watch was being mended so he used Ross's.
7. The play's ending was very good.
8. Mum's scales were broken so she used my sister's scales.
9. We used sticky tape to hold the pages together.
10. The chain's links were very strong and held the ship's anchor firmly.

Page 39

1. The butcher's shop is closed.
2. That is next year's calendar.
3. There are birds' nests in the beech trees.
4. Sandra dropped the speckled hen's egg.
5. This ship's sails are red.
6. My ski's clip is broken.
7. Some books' covers are torn.
8. The cricket team's score was high.

Page 40

1. Are policemen's heads the same shape as policemen's helmets?
2. The people's wishes must be carried out.
3. The women's changing rooms are cold.
4. He was a wolf in sheep's clothing.
5. Postmen's bags are often heavy.
6. It is difficult to see trout's eyes.
7. The cattle's lowing woke the Baby Jesus.

1. Sheep's wool often clings to fences.
2. The style of women's shoes is always changing.
3. Postmen's bicycles are often red.
4. The children's teacher always has an apple for lunch.

Practise Punctuation ~ Book 1
Answer pages

Page 41

1. William's coat is too big.
2. The boys' football team did well.
3. The firemen's hoses were tangled.
4. Somebody's watch has a loud alarm.
5. It was Nigel's fault.
6. Abraham's son was called Isaac.
7. It is hard to find bears' dens.
8. I clung to the horse's mane.
9. I can't remember the song's name.
10. She met me at my uncle's house.

Space it out

1. Harry's parrot is very clever.
2. I saw Luke's team win.
3. I nearly fell over the cliff's edge.
4. Jack's brother is good at maths.
5. The thieves' car broke down.
6. I went to the ladies' hairdresser.
7. That ruler's numbers are very faint.
8. Aeroplanes' cargoes are kept in the hold.

Page 43

1. The nurse's uniform was white.
2. Flamingoes' legs are very thin.
3. The conjuror's trick was very clever.
4. The attic's window is very small.
5. The two boys' diving belts were heavy.